A. Dublin street artists include fire jugglers.

B. Leaders of the 1916 Easter Rising were kept in
Kilmainham Jail.

C. When the weather is dry, Dubliners like to sip
their coffee at outdoor cafes.

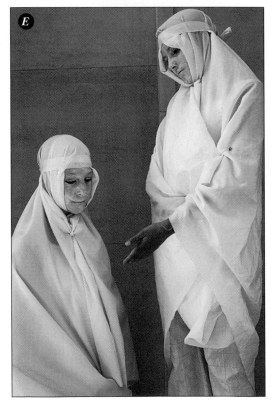

A. Dublin's many parks, such as People's Garden, hold concerts and exhibitions.

B. Dublin's double decker buses can carry twice as many passengers as regular buses.

C. O'Connell Bridge is named after Irish rights hero Daniel O'Connell.

D. Motorcyclists take a break during their tour of Dublin.

E. Mimes give a performance in downtown Dublin.

IRELAND
the land

Erinn Banting

A Bobbie Kalman Book
The Lands, Peoples, and Cultures Series

Crabtree Publishing Company

The Lands, Peoples, and Cultures Series

Created by Bobbie Kalman

Coordinating editor
Ellen Rodger

Project editor
P.A. Finlay

Production coordinator
Rosie Gowsell

Project development, photo research, and design
First Folio Resource Group, Inc.
Erinn Banting
Tom Dart
Greg Duhaney
Söğüt Y. Güleç
Debbie Smith

Editing
Carolyn Black

Prepress and printing
Worzalla Publishing Company

Consultants
Brian Costello; Dissolving Boundaries Through Technology in Education; Stephen Guidon; Matthew Keenan; Darren Kenny; Sean MacMathuna; Michael J. McCann, InfoMarex; Liam Merwick; Jennifer O'Connell and North Dublin National School Project's 5th class; Michael O'Gorman; Paul Quinn; Chris Stephenson; Colin Stephenson

Special Thanks
To Ivoane McMorough who connected us with her wonderful friends in Ireland. Thanks also to Patrick and Creena MacNeill who passed their love for Ireland on to Crabtree Publishing.

Photographs
Corbis/Magma Photo News Inc./Tom Bean: p. 25 (top); Corbis/Magma Photo News Inc./Richard Cummins: p. 17 (top), p. 24 (bottom); Corbis/Magma Photo News Inc./Macduff Everton: p. 25 (bottom); Corbis/Magma Photo News Inc./David Hosking: p. 28 (right); Corbis/Magma Photo News Inc./Ed Kashi: p. 13 (right); Corbis/Magma Photo News Inc./Alain Le Garsmeur: p. 26 (right); Corbis/Magma Photo News Inc./David Muench: p. 3; Corbis/Magma Photo News Inc./Tim Page: p. 22 (bottom); Corbis/Magma Photo News Inc./Carl Purcell: p. 18 (left); Corbis/Magma Photo News Inc./Michael Rose: p. 31; Corbis/Magma Photo News Inc./Joseph Sohm: p. 14 (top); Corbis/Magma Photo News Inc./Michael St. Maur Sheil: p. 27 (right); Corbis/Magma Photo News Inc./Geray Sweeney: p. 19, p. 28 (left); Corbis/Magma Photo News Inc./Michael S. Yamashita: p. 17 (bottom); Marc Crabtree: title page, front endpages page 1 (bottom two), page 2 (top, middle), page 3 (top left, bottom left, bottom right) rear endpages page 1 (top, bottom), page 3 (all), p.4 (bottom), p. 7 (both), p. 8 (bottom), p. 10, p. 12 (bottom), p. 13 (bottom), p. 15 (top), p. 16 (top), p. 21 (top), p. 22 (top), p. 23 (bottom), p. 24 (top), p. 30 (top); Peter Crabtree: cover, front endpages page 1 (top), page 2 (bottom right), page 3 (middle left, top right), rear endpages page 1 (middle), page 2 (all), p. 4 (top), p. 5 (both), p. 8 (top), p. 15 (bottom), p. 16 (bottom), p. 21 (bottom), p. 26 (bottom), p. 30 (inset); Peter Matthews: p. 11, p. 14 (bottom); Larry Nicholson/Photo Researchers: p. 29; Richard T. Nowitz/Photo Researchers: p. 20; Tim Thompson: p. 9, p. 12 (top), p. 18 (right), p. 23 (top), p. 27 (left)

Map
Jim Chernishenko

Illustrations
Dianne Eastman: icon
David Wysotski, Allure Illustrations: back cover

Cover: Gulls take refuge on the rocky, mossy cliffs on the coast of Ireland.

Title page: The harbor and sandy beaches of Ballycastle in Northern Ireland make the resort town popular with tourists.

Icon: A shamrock, or three-leaf clover, appears at the head of each section.

Back cover: Irish hares can most often be seen at night eating grasses and chewing at young trees with their large front teeth.

Published by
Crabtree Publishing Company

PMB 16A,
350 Fifth Avenue
Suite 3308
New York
N.Y. 10118

612 Welland Avenue
St. Catharines
Ontario, Canada
L2M 5V6

73 Lime Walk
Headington
Oxford OX3 7AD
United Kingdom

Cataloging in Publication Data
Banting, Erinn.
    Ireland the land / Erinn Banting.
        v. cm. -- (Lands, peoples, and cultures series)
Includes index.
    Contents: Land divided -- The Emerald Isle -- The Irish people -- Capital cities -- Growing cities -- From land and sea -- Industry, past and present -- Getting from place to place -- Island wildlife.
        ISBN 0-7787-9349-4 (RLB) -- ISBN 0-7787-9717-1 (pbk.)
    1. Ireland--Description and travel--Juvenile literature. [1. Ireland.] I. Title. II. Series.
DA978.2 .B36 2002
941.5--dc21
                                                    2001007747
                                                    LC

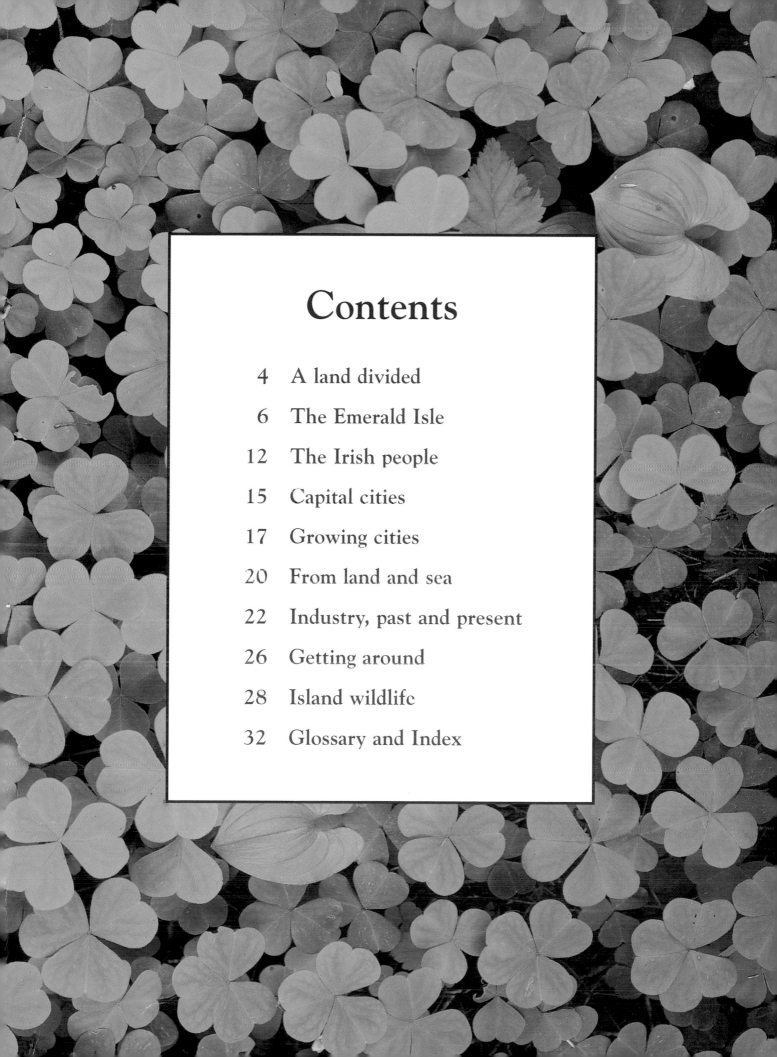

Contents

The island of Ireland lies off the west coast of the United Kingdom. It is bordered on the north, west, and south by the Atlantic Ocean, and on the east by the Irish Sea. Ireland is home to the Republic of Ireland, or Éire, which is an **independent** country, and Northern Ireland, which is a province of the United Kingdom.

Nearly five million people share the green fields, rugged mountains, and magnificent coasts of Ireland. People use the rich farmland on the island's large central plain to grow crops and raise sheep or cattle. Until about 30 years ago, farming was one of the largest industries in Ireland. Today, growing industries such as computer manufacturing are just as important to the **economy**.

(left) Students rest and study next to Fusiliers Arch, the entrance to St. Stephen's Green, Dublin's most popular park.

(below) Building murals are popular in some Belfast neighborhoods. This house is painted to show loyalty to the United Kingdom. The curb is also painted red, white, and blue, the colors of the British flag.

Troubled times

Ireland's history has not been peaceful. Since the 1100s, **Britain** has ruled all or part of the island. Irish resistance to foreign control grew stronger in the early 1900s when Irish **nationalists** organized political revolts against British rule. The south of Ireland gained full independence in 1949 and became the Republic of Ireland. Northern Ireland remained part of the United Kingdom.

Some people in the north were happy to remain part of the United Kingdom. Others wanted to be united with the Republic of Ireland. These differences led to violence between the two groups. While most of the fighting between the two groups has taken place in Northern Ireland, the people, economy, and culture of the whole island have suffered. After changes to the Republic's **constitution** in 1999 and agreements made by the British and Irish governments, the Irish are working together toward peace.

A ship carries goods to a Belfast port. With Ireland surrounded by water, there are ports on every coast.

(below) Bobby Sands died after going on a 65 day hunger strike. He was protesting British rule in Northern Ireland. Sands is a hero in some areas.

EVERYONE, REPUBLICAN OR OTHERWISE, HAS THEIR OWN PARTICULAR ROLE TO PLAY

...OUR REVENGE WILL BE THE LAUGHTER OF OUR CHILDREN

ROIBEAIRD O SEACHNASAIGH
BOBBY SANDS
IRISH REPUBLICAN
REVOLUTIONARY, POET, GAEILGEOIR, VISIONARY
54-1981

People often call Ireland the "Emerald Isle" because of its rich green landscapes. The island, which is about 32,331 square miles (83,737 square kilometers), consists of a large central plain surrounded by low mountains. The Republic of Ireland stretches across five-sixths of the land, while Northern Ireland covers one-sixth of the land. **Inlets**, bays, and **peninsulas** dot the coasts. Off the north, south, and west coasts lie smaller islands, such as the Aran Islands in the west.

The Ice Age

A hundred thousand years ago, the British Isles, which include England, Scotland, Wales, and Ireland, were connected to Europe by a land bridge, or giant strip of land. This was during the Ice Age, when the land was frozen and covered by glaciers, or large, slow-moving chunks of ice. When the glaciers melted around 8000 B.C., water covered the land bridge and separated the British Isles from the rest of Europe. The North Channel and the Irish Sea separated Ireland from the other British Isles.

The central plain

The melted glaciers left a rich layer of soil that extends across the middle of Ireland. This lowland area, called the central plain, is mostly farmland rich in a mineral called **limestone**. Limestone makes it easy to grow root vegetables, such as carrots, potatoes, and sugar beets, and grass for **livestock** to feed on.

Mountains

Low mountain ranges form a circle around the central plain. The main ranges are the Donegal Mountains in the northwest, the Wicklow Mountains in the east, the Mountains of Connemara in the west, and the Mountains of Kerry in the southwest.

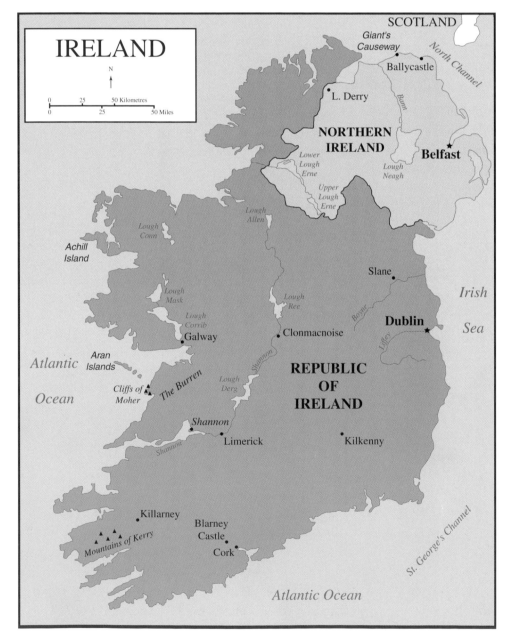

IRELAND

N

0   25   50 Kilometres
0   25   50 Miles

SCOTLAND
Giant's Causeway
Ballycastle
North Channel
L. Derry
Bann
NORTHERN IRELAND
Lower Lough Erne
Lough Neagh
Belfast
Upper Lough Erne
Lough Allen
Lough Conn
Achill Island
Lough Mask
Lough Corrib
Galway
Lough Ree
Slane
Boyne
Irish
Dublin
Liffey
Sea
Clonmacnoise
Aran Islands
Atlantic
Ocean
Shannon
Cliffs of Moher
The Burren
Lough Derg
REPUBLIC OF IRELAND
Shannon
Limerick
Kilkenny
Shannon
St. George's Channel
Killarney
Blarney Castle
Mountains of Kerry
Cork
Atlantic Ocean

A farmer plows his land to prepare it for planting.

A pile of peat has been cut from the land. Peat comes from wet, swampy lands, called bogs. Some peat lands are so deep and wet you cannot walk on them.

Drumlins

Small, rocky hills, called drumlins, run along the border between Northern Ireland and the Republic of Ireland. The drumlins formed after the Ice Age, when melting glaciers deposited rocks on the ground.

Peat bogs

Peat bogs cover about fifteen percent of the farmland in central and western Ireland. The bogs were originally shallow lakes that did not drain properly. Instead, the lakes filled up with mud, plants, and mosses. Over thousands of years, the plants and mosses died and sank to the bottom of the lakes. As they were covered and flattened by more layers of dead plants and mosses, they formed a spongy material called peat or turf.

Gradually, layers of peat built up and filled entire lakes, forming the bogs. Plants, such as sphagnum moss, and insects, such as dragonflies, live in peat bogs. In parts of rural Ireland, some people use peat to heat their homes, although it is becoming less common. Most of Ireland's peat is harvested from the Bog of Allen, in the centre of the Republic of Ireland. The Bog of Allen is the largest group of bogs in the country, extending 375 square miles (970 square kilometers).

Rivers and *loughs*

The River Shannon is the longest river in Ireland, at 240 miles (386 kilometers). Beginning in north central Ireland, the river flows south until it reaches the Atlantic Ocean. It travels through three major *loughs,* or lakes — Lough Allen, Lough Ree, and Lough Derg. Many smaller rivers, such as the River Liffey and River Boyne, are scattered across Ireland.

The largest lake in Ireland is Lough Neagh, which lies in Northern Ireland. It measures 153 square miles (396 square kilometers). Not quite as large as Lough Neagh is a group of lakes called the Lakes of Killarney, which are famous for their beauty. The three lakes — Lower Lake, Middle Lake, and Upper Lake — stretch among the mountains and forests of Killarney National Park, a **nature reserve** in the Republic of Ireland.

(below) The Carrick-a-rede Rope Bridge over this gorge on the north coast of Ireland is 25 meters (80 feet) above the water.

(above) Ireland's rocky coasts and cliffs are a favorite spot for seabirds to rest.

On the coasts

Each coast of Ireland has distinct features. Steep cliffs, made of limestone and granite, a type of very hard rock, rise on the west coast and drop sharply into the sea. The northeast coast is also rugged, with rocky, weather-beaten cliffs. Lying between the cliffs are **fertile**, green valleys, called glens. The Wicklow Mountains extend along the east coast. They shelter peat bogs, animals, such as ravens and foxes, and plants, including the sessile oak. The sessile oak, which is the Republic of Ireland's national tree, can live for a thousand years. The south coast is known for its peninsulas and bays, including Mizen Head Peninsula, Sheep's Head Peninsula, and Iveragh Peninsula.

Even though the Macgillicuddy Reeks have eroded, they are still home to Ireland's highest peak, Carrauntoohill. It rises to a height of 3,414 feet (1,041 meters).

The Ring of Kerry

Iveragh Peninsula is famous for the Ring of Kerry, a ring-shaped area with marshlands, rugged shores, sandy beaches, and strange rock formations, such as the Skellig Rock. The Skellig Rock is a big rock that looks like a pile of smaller rocks stacked on top of one another.

In the Ring of Kerry stand the majestic Macgillicuddy Reeks, part of the Mountains of Kerry. A reek is a mountain that is millions of years old that has **eroded**, becoming smaller over time.

The Giant's Causeway

Off the north coast of Ireland is a group of rock formations called the Giant's Causeway. The Causeway looks like a long road made of more than 40,000 six-sided columns of basalt, a type of volcanic rock. About 60 million years ago, hot lava flowed from volcanoes in the area. When the lava touched the sea, it cooled and formed layers of hard basalt. Over time, the basalt shifted and broke into six-sided columns.

The columns of the Giant's Causeway stretch from the northern shore into the North Channel. Across the North Channel, off the coast of Scotland, is a similar group of rock formations. According to Irish legend, a giant named Fionn MacCumhaill built the Causeway so he could cross the North Channel to Scotland.

Each column in the Giant's Causeway is between 15 and 20 inches (38 and 51 centimeters) wide.

Ireland's islands

Several small islands lie off Ireland's west coast, including Achill Island, Valentia Island, and Tory Island. Very few people live on these islands because little vegetation grows there and the land is difficult to farm. More people live on the Aran Islands, a group of three islands named Inishmore, Inishmaan, and Inisheer, also off the west coast.

Many people on the Aran Islands live as their **ancestors** did hundreds of years ago. Their homes have walls made of stone and roofs made of thatch, or tightly woven straw. Instead of wood or metal fences, islanders divide their properties with walls made from piles of rocks.

Wet and windy

One reason why Ireland is so green is that it rains between 175 and 200 days each year. Often, the rain is not very heavy and falls in a mist. The Irish call these misty days "soft days." In some parts of Ireland, the weather can change from rainy to sunny very suddenly because high winds blowing in from the Atlantic Ocean push away the clouds. Sometimes, the winds blow up to 80 miles (130 kilometers) per hour.

The west coast and the islands off the west coast receive more wind than the mainland because they are not sheltered from the high winds and water from the Atlantic Ocean. Fishers on the coast wear wool sweaters that are oiled to protect them from the wet, gusty weather.

Not too hot, not too cold

Ireland is never very hot or very cold. The reason for Ireland's year-round mild climate is that it lies in the path of the Gulf Stream, a warm current of water that flows from the Gulf of Mexico, along the east coast of the United States, and through the Atlantic Ocean to Ireland. In some parts of Ireland, such as the southwest coast, the Gulf Stream even allows palm trees and other tropical plants to grow.

Despite the rain, a family enjoys a picnic at a park in Cushendall, a town on the north coast of Northern Ireland.

If you ask people in Ireland where they live, they are likely to name the county they are from rather than the city, town, or village. For example, they might say, "I come from County Cork" or "I come from County Tipperary." There are six counties in Northern Ireland and twenty-six counties in the Republic of Ireland. These counties make up Ireland's four provinces — Ulster, in the north; Leinster, in the east; Munster, in the south; and Connaught, in the west.

The Celts and Vikings

Many Irish people trace their ancestry back to the Celts and Vikings. The Celts, or Gaels, came to Ireland from Europe around 300 B.C. and controlled the island until around 795 A.D., when Vikings from Scandinavia arrived. Although the Vikings gained control over most of the island by 835, the language of the Celts, Gaelic, continued to be spoken and Celtic traditions were still celebrated. Today, Gaelic is one of the official languages of the Republic of Ireland, and the Irish people still celebrate Celtic festivals from thousands of years ago.

(above) Many families in Ireland are large, with four or five children.

(below) Students must learn the Gaelic language in the Republic of Ireland.

The English

Some Irish people trace their ancestry to the English, who first came to Ireland in the 1100s. The English imposed their laws and customs, and took over most of the land that the Celts had settled. English and Celtic people married one another and began families. The **descendants** of many of these families still live in the homes that their ancestors have owned for hundreds of years.

The Ulster Scots

The region of Ulster is made up of nine counties, six of which form Northern Ireland. The other three counties are part of the Republic of Ireland. England wanted to **colonize** Ireland, and in the 1500s and 1600s, the English monarchy offered people from England and Scotland free land in Ulster. The lands, which had belonged to the Irish, were known as "plantations" because the English and Scottish were "planted" there. People descended from the Ulster Scots still live in Northern Ireland. In parts of Belfast, a city where many people of Scottish descent live, street signs are in English and Scottish Gaelic, a language of Scotland.

This man is a descendant of the Ulster Scots who came to the north of Ireland in the 1600s.

At a parade in Belfast, two women show their support for Northern Ireland's union with Britain by wearing skirts and carrying umbrellas decorated with the Union Jack, the flag of Britain.

Roman Catholics and Protestants

In the 1500s, the majority of people in Ireland were Roman Catholics. Roman Catholicism is a **denomination** of Christianity, a religion based on the teachings of Jesus Christ. Christians believe that Christ is the son of God. In 1533, England's King Henry VIII adopted another denomination of Christianity called Protestantism as his religion. He then declared Protestantism the official religion of England and Ireland.

Most Irish Catholics refused to convert, or change their religion. Some Catholics in the north agreed to convert to Protestantism in order to keep their land and rights. Other people in the north from England and Scotland were already Protestants. The differences in religion caused fighting, especially in Northern Ireland. There have been political differences, too. For many years, the Protestants in Northern Ireland wished to remain part of the United Kingdom, while the Roman Catholics of Northern Ireland and the Republic thought that Northern Ireland should be reunited with the Republic. Today, both Protestants and Catholics are trying to live together in peace.

(above) People all over the world celebrate their Irish backgrounds. Three friends from New York City carry a flag of the Republic of Ireland to show their Irish heritage during a St. Patrick's Day parade.

(below) Two friends enjoy ice cream cones together on O'Connell Street, in Dublin.

The Irish abroad

From 1845 to 1849, a disease destroyed Ireland's potato crops and caused a **famine**. The Irish called the famine *an gorta mór*, which means "the great hunger." Nearly 800,000 people who relied on the potato as the main part of their diet died of starvation or diseases caused by not eating nutritious food. More than one million Irish emigrated, or moved, from Ireland to other countries, such as the United States, England, Canada, and Australia, in search of a better life. In the 1900s, political problems, war, and violence in Northern Ireland caused millions more to leave Ireland.

Today, millions of people around the world consider themselves to be Irish, or of Irish descent. They celebrate Irish festivals, tell Irish tales, and sing and dance to traditional Irish music. As tensions in Ireland lessen, many descendants of Irish emigrants are returning to their homeland. People from countries in Europe, such as France, Germany, and Spain, are also moving to Ireland to work.

North of the River Liffey

Old buildings are common sights in northern Dublin. One of the most important buildings is the General Post Office. It became famous after the Easter Rising, a **rebellion** against British rule that took place in 1916. Padraig Pearse, James Connolly, and other leaders of the Irish Volunteers, a nationalist group, stood on the front steps of the General Post Office and declared independence from Britain. Today, a memorial in the building honors the people who died in the Easter Rising, and oil paintings in the building depict scenes from the battle.

To the south

Southern Dublin is more modern than northern Dublin, with highways and shopping malls in addition to **restored** older buildings. Southern Dublin is home to the Christ Church Cathedral. Built in 1172, it is the oldest church in Dublin. An old burial room beneath the cathedral's floor holds an unusual artifact — the skeleton of a cat found in one of the pipes of the church's organ! Southern Dublin is also home to a large park called Phoenix Park. People can escape the busy city life by visiting the park's gardens and nature trails.

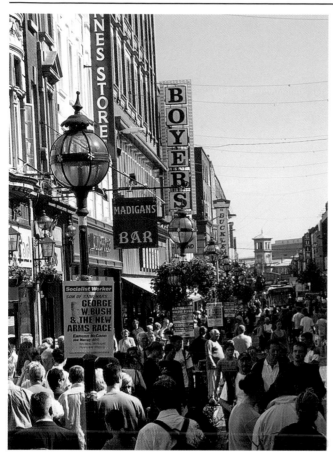

Grafton Street is one of Dublin's busiest streets. Pedestrians can move easily from the large department stores to the small boutiques and specialty shops because no cars are allowed on Grafton Street.

Dublin, on the east coast, is the largest city in Ireland. It has been the **capital** of the Republic of Ireland since 1922. The Vikings founded the city in 841 A.D. on the banks of the River Liffey. They called it *dubh linn*, which means "the dark pool." During the 1700s, Dublin expanded to include land on the south side of the River Liffey. Today, the river divides the city into northern Dublin and southern Dublin.

The Custom House lies along the River Liffey. It was the first big government building in Dublin. The exterior features sculptures representing Ireland's rivers.

A view of Belfast City Hall from Donegall Square, the business and shopping district of Belfast.

Belfast

Belfast is Northern Ireland's capital and its largest city. It is also the second largest city in Ireland. Surrounded by hills and ancient castles, Belfast sits at the mouth of the River Lagan, on the northeast coast. Belfast's name comes from the Gaelic phrase *béal feirste,* which means "mouth of the Feirste," a stream that joins the River Lagan.

In the 1800s, Belfast became a center for textile manufacturing and shipbuilding, and the city quickly grew into a busy **port**. The most well known shipyard in Belfast's history, Harland and Wolff, is still in operation. It is where the famous ship the *Titanic* was built in 1912.

Rebuilding the city

As the center of British rule in Northern Ireland, Belfast has been the site of violent clashes between Roman Catholics and Protestants. Life in Belfast is very different from life in other Irish cities. Many neighborhoods are segregated, or divided, into areas where either Roman Catholics or Protestants live. Until recently, cars were searched before they were allowed in downtown Belfast because **terrorist** groups frequently hid bombs in them.

The government of Northern Ireland is trying to improve life in Belfast and make it a safer place to live. New homes are being built to replace older apartments and houses that were destroyed by vandalism.

The grounds of Belfast City Hall, built during 1898 - 1906, features a statue of Britain's Queen Victoria who died in 1901.

Ireland's largest cities are among the fastest growing places in the world. Many of them have both ancient and modern areas, where brand new buildings stand near castles, towers, and forts that are centuries old.

Cork

Cork, on the south coast, is the second largest city in the Republic. Its name comes from the Gaelic word *corcaigh*, which means "marshy land." Around 600 A.D., Cork developed around an ancient **monastery** called St. Finbar. Today, it is a port and a busy center for computer and car manufacturing, food processing, and steel production. Many special events take place in Cork, such as the Cork Film Festival and Cork Jazz Festival, which are enjoyed by people from all over the world.

People stroll along High Street, in Kilkenny, in the southeast Republic. England's King James I declared Kilkenny a city in 1609.

Traders began using Cork's main port, Cork Harbor, hundreds of years ago. The harbor provided a safe place for their ships and cargo.

King John's Castle, in Limerick, was built beside the River Shannon, in an area that was difficult for invaders to reach.

Limerick

Limerick is another busy sea port, located on the banks of the River Shannon in the Republic of Ireland. Vikings founded the city in 900 A.D. It was later taken over by the **Normans**, who ruled England and most of Ireland beginning in the late 1100s.

The Normans divided Limerick into "English Town," where only British people were allowed to live, and "Irish Town," where only Irish people were allowed to live. "English Town" and "Irish Town" still exist in Limerick, but people from any background can live in either area. Parts of an old wall that once divided the English and Irish districts still stand next to the ruins of King John's Castle, which was built in 1210 for England's King. As well as Irish Town and English Town, Limerick has a third district called Newtown Pery, which is the modern downtown area.

A man reads his paper in Galway's Eyre Square. Built in 1710, the square was named after Edward Eyre, the mayor of Galway at the time. The square's name was changed in 1965 to Kennedy Memorial Square in honor of American president John F. Kennedy, who was of Irish descent.

Galway

Galway, on the west coast of the Republic, is one of the fastest growing cities in the **European Union** (EU). Computer manufacturers, such as COGNEX, from the United States; and Siemens, from Germany, are opening factories in the city and creating many new jobs.

Galway's culture is an interesting mix of Celtic and Spanish. More than any other major city in Ireland, Galway has maintained its Celtic arts, traditions, and language. The Spanish influence, which began when Spanish traders arrived in the city during the 1400s, can be seen in Galway's **architecture**. The Spanish Arch, where Spanish trading ships unloaded their cargo, still stands near the River Corrib. The arch, built in 1584, was added to a wall that Norman invaders built around the center of Galway in the 1200s to keep the Irish out. Sections of the wall remain today.

Houses, shops, and office buildings line the banks of the River Foyle in L. Derry.

L. Derry

For hundreds of years, people have disagreed on the name of L. Derry, a city in Northern Ireland. Roman Catholics call it Derry, while Protestants call it Londonderry. The name L. Derry softens the disagreement. L. Derry is the second largest city in Northern Ireland. Its name comes from the Gaelic word *doire*, which means "oak grove," because oak trees once grew in the area. Today, L. Derry is a manufacturing center for car parts and clothing.

L. Derry has the largest Roman Catholic population in Northern Ireland, and, like Belfast, many neighborhoods in the city are segregated. The outside walls of some buildings in these areas are covered with large paintings that represent the religious and political beliefs of their owners. These neighborhoods suffered a great deal of damage during decades of fighting between Roman Catholics and Protestants. Today, the government is paying to repair damaged buildings and build new homes. The people of L. Derry are also trying to stop the violence and make their city a safer place to live.

Fishing, raising livestock, and growing crops are important in both Northern Ireland and the Republic of Ireland. At one time, more people fished and farmed in the Republic. Northern Ireland's economy depended on other large industries, such as shipbuilding.

Thirty years ago, most fishing boats in the Republic were owned by individual families, and farms were small. Today, large farms, called cooperatives, are replacing many smaller farms. Cooperatives are owned by groups of farmers who share equally in the work and profits.

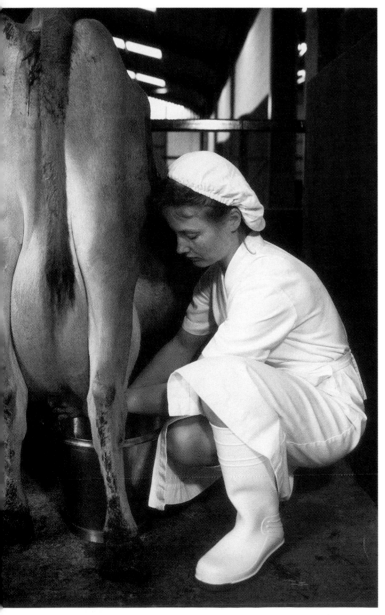

Fishing
Rich fishing areas surround Ireland, especially along the west coast. There, people fish for mackerel, herring, cod, and whiting, as well as scallops, mussels, and other types of shellfish. Fishers also catch salmon and trout in Ireland's many freshwater lakes and streams.

Cattle and sheep
Most farmers in Ireland raise livestock, especially cattle and sheep. Beef cattle feed on grasses on the central plain. Dairy cattle, which farmers use to produce milk, butter, and cheese, are raised in southern Ireland. There, the land is better for growing hay and straw, which the cattle eat. Sheep, which are used for wool and meat, are raised in the highland areas, especially along the west coast and in Northern Ireland. Sheep are able to survive on the rocky terrain because they need a smaller grazing area than cattle do.

Beginning in 1986, cattle from countries all over the world, including Northern Ireland and parts of the Republic of Ireland, were infected by an outbreak of mad cow disease. Cows infected by the disease became ill and died. Some human beings who ate meat from infected cows also became ill. By 2001, more than 180,000 cases of mad cow disease were recorded around the world. Hundreds of thousands of cattle were killed to prevent the disease from spreading to other animals and to humans. In Northern Ireland and the Republic, the **export** of meat and animals was halted. It was not until the threat of mad cow disease lessened that people felt comfortable again eating meat.

Cooperative creameries are becoming more common in Ireland. Individual farmers who own smaller dairy farms work together to build creameries where they sell milk, butter, and cheese.

The popularity of potatoes in Irish cooking makes it easy to sell "spuds" in Ireland. This woman delivers the root vegetable to customers in county Meath.

Growing potatoes

Irish farmers grow many root vegetables, such as potatoes, turnips, and sugar beets, which flourish in Ireland's wet climate. An English soldier and explorer named Sir Walter Raleigh is believed to have brought the first potatoes to Ireland in the 1580s. The vegetable quickly became the most important crop in the country. Before the potato famine, one-third of Ireland's people relied solely on the potato for food.

In the spring, Irish farmers plant potatoes in long rows. They then pile dirt over the rows to protect the potatoes from the sun. In the fall, machines called diggers dig the potatoes out of the ground. The potatoes are left in the fields in rows, called windrows, until another machine called a harvester picks them up.

This livestock farmer, with the help of his sheepdog, raises sheep for their wool and for export to other countries. Ireland's large open fields provide excellent grazing pastures for Ireland's sheep.

Today, Ireland's main manufacturing exports are chemicals, pharmaceuticals, and computer parts. With a small population, Ireland's economy depends on trade with other countries.

Northern Ireland and the Republic of Ireland have two separate economies. Northern Ireland's economy was traditionally more industrial because of its ties to Britain. Goods such as livestock, crops, textiles, steel, ships, and ship parts were sold to Britain, which then exported these items all over the world.

After many years of violence in Northern Ireland, the strong economy suffered. Many companies were forced to shut down, and foreign companies did not want to open there. Now, as the area becomes more peaceful, new businesses, such as IBM, a computer company which is based in the United States, are opening in Northern Ireland.

Industry in the Republic

Industry and trade in the Republic have improved since it joined the European Union in 1973. The Republic now exports goods to Europe, the United States, Canada, and Japan. Manufacturers from other countries, including tire company Michelin, based in France, and electronics company Ericsson, based in Sweden, have also opened factories in Ireland.

The Ford Motor Company, based in the United States, has a plant in Northern Ireland where people make car parts.

Linen

Linen is a fabric that has been woven in Ireland since the late 1600s, when a group of **immigrants** from France came to Ireland. Many of the immigrants, who had worked as weavers in France, settled in Antrim, an area in Northern Ireland. There, they grew flax, a type of plant. The stem of flax has small fibers that the weavers spun into thread and used to make linen. They sold the fabric at fairs called Brown Linen Halls, where people also bought clothing, bed sheets, and other items made from linen. Today, linen is still produced in Northern Ireland and in northern parts of the Republic, such as Donegal.

Wool

Wool made in Northern Ireland and the Republic of Ireland is known for its durability. People around the world use it to knit heavy sweaters, blankets, coats, and mittens. Brightly colored wool is also woven through black, gray, or brown wool to make a thick fabric called tweed. Tweed, with its small spots of color, is used to make hats, coats, pants, skirts, and other articles of clothing.

The Irish are famous for their linen handkerchiefs, tablecloths, and clothing, which are decorated with hand-embroidered patterns.

Visitors can buy Irish wool products from a wool factory or a wool shop. This man sells Irish wool sweaters to tourists at the Cliffs of Mohr.

Take a flashlight and adult if you venture into the dungeons of Blarney Castle. The castle's dark, underground cells were once used to keep prisoners.

Tourism

Tourism is one of Ireland's fastest-growing industries. Ireland's ancient monasteries, tombs, castles, and other historic sites are popular with tourists. Some visitors even stay in castles that have been renovated and turned into hotels. Tourists also relax on the coasts, hike through national parks, visit local shops, and stop by pubs for a snack.

Waterford crystal

In 1783, the Waterford Glass House opened in Waterford, a city on the southeast coast of the Republic of Ireland. It soon became one of the best known manufacturers of crystal in the world. Crystal is a type of glass with minerals added to it. The minerals make the glass sparkle when it reflects light. Glass blowers use very long, metal poles, which look like giant straws, to blow the crystal into different objects, such as glasses, vases, bowls, and pitchers. After the crystal is blown, cutters carve intricate designs and shapes onto its surface. The crystal made in Waterford is known for its beautiful, detailed designs, and is popular among people who collect fine crystal.

(below) A cutter decorates a crystal vase at the Waterford factory.

Connemara marble, which is mined from the Connemara mountains, is a type of green rock with streaks of white, beige, or brown. People use it to make jewelry or to decorate important buildings.

Powering Ireland

In some parts of rural Ireland, people still harvest peat and use it as fuel to heat factories and homes. Gathering peat is called "footing the turf." People called cutters dig up the peat from peat bogs using a slane, which looks like a shovel. Then, the peat is cut into bricks. Any excess water is squeezed out of the bricks, which are stacked into piles and left in the sun to dry.

In some places, cutters use more modern machinery to harvest peat. This equipment allows them to remove larger blocks of peat than they can using slanes. The big slabs are taken to processing plants, where machines crush them into a powder. When the powder is almost completely dry, it is pressed into bricks. People buy the bricks to heat their homes.

Burning peat

Unfortunately, burning peat is extremely harmful to the environment. It releases carbon dioxide and methane gas into the air, which contributes to pollution. Some cities, such as Dublin, no longer allow people to burn peat because it causes pollution. Companies are now finding ways to make synthetic, or artificial, peat. When synthetic peat is burned, it does not create as much smoke and ash as natural peat does. Synthetic peat also saves the natural peat bogs for the plants and animals that live in them.

Cutters dig up blocks of peat at a bog in Gleniff, a town in the west of the Republic.

Getting around

Throughout many parts of Ireland, roads that are only wide enough for one car wind through the countryside. Sheep from nearby fields sometimes wander onto these roads, slowing down vehicles. Traffic moves even more slowly in cities, where pedestrians, cars, bicycles, and buses crowd the streets. The government has built new highways to accommodate the large number of vehicles coming through Ireland's cities every day. The *Bus atha Cliath,* or Dublin Bus, uses double-decker buses to carry more passengers, especially during rush hour. In Belfast, long concertina buses carry people on their way to work. They are called concertina buses because they have a rubber section in the middle that looks like a concertina, or small accordion. The rubber section helps the buses turn corners.

Taxis

Taxis are a popular way of getting around. People can hail, or call, taxis in the street. Special taxis, called "hackneys," cannot be hailed, but must be ordered by phone or at private offices, where a price for the ride is agreed on in advance.

(above) What types of transportation do you see in this photograph of Dublin?

In some cities in Northern Ireland, such as Belfast and L. Derry, there is more than one type of taxi. Public taxis share the road with private taxis, called black taxis. Black taxis began operating in Roman Catholic neighborhoods during the 1960s. At that time, the fighting in Northern Ireland was very bad and the public bus system closed. Roman Catholic taxi drivers started driving people from one Roman Catholic neighborhood to another. Today, black taxis are mainly used for tours around the city, and people of any religion can use one.

A Belfast taxi driver waits to pick up a passenger. Black taxis are common in Northern Ireland. A black taxi fare is usually very cheap.

Steamships and *curraghs*

People on the Aran Islands rely on water transportation to get to and from the mainland. Special boats, called steamships, carry food, mail, people, and supplies from the mainland to a port on the island of Inishmore.

For 100 years, *curraghs* have transported people and supplies to the other two Aran Islands, Inishmaan and Inisheer. A *curragh* is a small boat made of canvas stretched over a wooden frame. To make a *curragh* waterproof, the canvas is covered in thick, black tar. People push the *curraghs* through the water with narrow paddles.

Ireland's ports handle more than 45,000 tons of goods in one year.

Many ports

As well as traveling over land, people in Ireland travel through the air and on the water. Ireland has several large airports, and ferry service runs from several ports. Nearly every major city and town on Ireland's coasts has a port. Ireland depends on its ports for survival. Textiles, food, and other merchandise are shipped in large containers to other countries, and cargo ships from other countries bring supplies and food to Ireland's ports. Once the goods arrive in Ireland, large trucks transport them across the country.

Island transportation

Transportation on the Aran Islands is not as modern as it is in other parts of Ireland. Bus and train service does not exist, and only a few automobiles can be seen on the roads. Instead, many islanders travel in jaunting cars, which are four-wheeled wagons that are pulled by a horse.

(below) **Some** *curraghs* *have motors so that they can move more quickly through the water. In shallow water, long poles are used to push the* **curraghs.**

Along Ireland's coasts, plants, such as sea pinks and bladder campions, thrive despite the rough winds and saltwater blowing in from the ocean. In the bogs, flowering plants, such as heather and bog asphodel, attract butterflies and dragonflies. Another bog plant that attracts insects is the common sundew. The tiny hairs that grow on the surface of the sundew's leaves are dangerous. Insects that come into contact with the hairs stick to the leaves, which then trap the bugs.

Shamrocks

Shamrock is a common name for the three-leaf **clovers** that grow in Ireland, including white clovers, red clovers, and black medics. The green clover, which is one of Ireland's national symbols, is the most common and best known. Some people believe that finding a four-leaf green clover, which is much rarer than a three-leaf green clover, brings good luck.

Birds

Birds flock to Ireland's coasts. Some are native to Ireland, such as kittiwakes, a type of gull. Kittiwakes build their nests from seaweed and attach it to the sides of steep cliffs with their droppings! Other birds from around the world migrate to Ireland during the winter because of Ireland's year-round mild climate.

Not as many birds live on Ireland's central plain because so few trees grow there. Some, such as yellow hammers, jackdaws, willow warblers, and wrens live in hedgerows, which are walls made from shrubs that divide properties.

The sundew plant gets its food from the insects it catches and kills.

Kestrels are small birds with brownish-red feathers that let them blend in with surrounding bog areas. Kestrels can nest on the ground without being seen, and can sneak up on small rodents, frogs, and dragonflies.

Animals on the plain

Animals such as bank voles and rabbits live underground in large burrows, or tunnels. Hedgerows shelter the burrows, so the animals can come and go without being seen by their predators, or other animals that eat them. Irish hares sometimes live in burrows, but usually they live on a form, which is a flat, oval-shaped patch of vegetation. Irish hares look like rabbits, but have much longer legs and ears that give them speed and better hearing to escape from their predators. They are also larger than rabbits. The average Irish hare grows to 13 pounds (6 kilograms) and 25 inches (63 centimeters) long. Ireland's smaller islands have large colonies of hares, which can often be seen running along the beaches.

No snakes!

Ireland is one of the few places in the world where snakes do not live. In fact, they have not lived there since the Ice Age! When the land froze over, it became too cold for snakes to survive. After the glaciers melted, the water prevented new species of snakes from crossing into Ireland from the other British Isles.

Many people in Ireland believe that it was not the Ice Age, but Saint Patrick, the **patron saint** of Ireland, who got rid of Ireland's snakes. According to a popular tale, snakes lived in Ireland until Saint Patrick climbed to the top of a mountain and rang a large bell, which scared them all away.

Common seals and gray seals lie on the sunny beaches and shores. Seals live mainly on land, but swim in the water to search for food. Gray seals eat up to thirteen pounds (six kilograms) of fish every day. Luckily, Ireland's coastal waters are full of fish.

The Burren

Ireland has many nature reserves. One reserve, on the west coast, is the Burren. The Burren is a large limestone **plateau** covered by boulders and unusual rock formations. Its name comes from the Gaelic word *boireann*, which means "rocky land." More than 1,000 types of plants and flowers grow among the hollows and cracks of the Burren. Some plants, such as mountain avens, are alpine plants, which means that they grow in cold climates. They peak out of hollows that form when water and wind erode parts of the plateau. Other plants, such as maidenhair avens, are Mediterranean plants, which means that they are usually found in warmer climates. These plants grow in cracks, called gyrkes. Caves beneath the plateau store warm air, which blows up through the gyrkes and keeps the plants warm.

*(opposite, inset) **An abandoned stone cottage on the Burren.***

*(opposite) **On the Burren, thousands of types of plants grow among the many limestone boulders and rocks.***

Lough Hyne

Lough Hyne is an inland sea in southern Ireland. An inland sea forms when a freshwater lake gradually erodes below sea level. Instead of draining its water into the ocean, the lake draws saltwater in from the ocean. As Lough Hyne eroded and filled with saltwater, marine animals that normally live in the ocean were drawn into the lake along with the water.

Today, Lough Hyne is a nature reserve. Among its strange inhabitants are more than 150 species of sea sponges. Sea sponges are animals that look like plants because of the many feeders, or arms, that branch out around them. Sponges do not move, but attach themselves to rocky surfaces beneath the water and absorb food through their feeders.

Other strange fish in the waters of Lough Hyne are triggerfish, pipefish, sea squirts, jellyfish, and gobies. A goby has two fins that join underneath its body to form a suction cup. The suction cup allows it to cling to rocky surfaces and feed along the bottom of the *lough*.

Glossary

ancestor A person from whom one is descended

architecture The science and art of designing and constructing buildings

Britain An island with a group of countries including England, Scotland, and Wales

capital A city where the government of a state or country is located

clover A plant with leaves of three or four leaflets and small, rounded flowers

colonize To establish a settlement in a distant country

constitution The set of laws that govern a country

denomination An organized religious group within a faith

descendant A person who can trace his or her family roots to a certain family or group

economy The organization and management of a country's businesses, industry, and money

erode To wear away gradually, as with wind and rain wearing away mountain peaks

European Union An organization of fifteen European countries that work together to promote trade among themselves and the rest of the world

export To sell goods to another country

famine An extreme shortage of food in a country

fertile Able to produce abundant crops or vegetation

immigrant A person who settles in another country

independent Not governed by a foreign power

inlet A narrow body of water leading inland from a larger body of water

limestone A rock used for building

livestock Farm animals

monastery A building where monks or nuns live and work according to religious rules

nationalist A person who wants his or her country to be independent

nature reserve A park where wildlife is protected from hunters and is observed by scientists and tourists

Normans A group of people who came from France and conquered England

patron saint A saint who is believed to protect a person, profession, city, or country

peat A rich soil made up of decaying plants in bogs and marshes

peninsula An area of land that is surrounded by water on three sides

plateau An area of flat land that is higher than the surrounding land

port A place where ships load and unload cargo

rebellion An uprising against a government

restore To bring something back to its original condition

terrorist Using extreme violence, often for political reasons

United Kingdom A group of countries including England, Scotland, Wales, and Northern Ireland

Index

1 2 3 4 5 6 7 8 9 0   Printed in the USA   5 4 3 2

Belfast

A. Protestants and Catholics identify their neighborhoods with murals. This is a Protestant neighborhood.

B. Belfast's rebuilding includes a modern waterfront.

C. The boat builders, Harland & Wolff, built the Titanic in Belfast in 1912.

The Irish countryside

A. While some horses are trained to race, others are used on farms.

B. A person who takes care of horses is called a groom. He is trying to keep this great horse in his stall.

C. A cart with two wheels and a horse is called a sulky. This farmer is driving up the lane to his home.